STEPHEN J. ROSE is a nationally recognized labor economist. Currently, he is a research professor at the George Washington Institute of Public Policy and a nonresident fellow at the Urban Institute. He previously held senior positions at Educational Testing Service, the U.S. Department of Labor, the U.S. Congress Joint Economic Committee, the National Commission for Employment Policy, and the Washington State senate. His commentaries have appeared in the *New York Times*, the *Washington Post*, the *Wall Street Journal*, and other print and broadcast media. The author of *Rebound: Why America Will Emerge Stronger from the Financial Crisis* and *Social Stratification in the United States: The American Profile Poster* (The New Press), he lives in Washington, DC.

ALSO BY STEPHEN J. ROSE

Rebound:
Why America Will Emerge Stronger from the Financial Crisis

Social Stratification in the United States

*The American Profile Poster
of Who Owns What,
Who Makes How Much, and
Who Works Where*

STEPHEN J. ROSE

NEW YORK   LONDON

Requests for permission to reproduce selections from this book should be made through our website: https://thenewpress.com/contact.

Published in the United States by The New Press, New York, 2022
Distributed by Two Rivers Distribution

ISBN 978-1-62097-740-8 (paperback)
ISBN 978-1-62097-764-4 (ebook)
CIP data is available

The New Press publishes books that promote and enrich public discussion and understanding of the issues vital to our democracy and to a more equitable world. These books are made possible by the enthusiasm of our readers; the support of a committed group of donors, large and small; the collaboration of our many partners in the independent media and the not-for-profit sector; booksellers, who often hand-sell New Press books; librarians; and above all by our authors.

www.thenewpress.com

Book design and composition by Lovedog Studio
This book was set in Sabon Monotype

Printed in the United States of America

2 4 6 8 10 9 7 5 3 1

Contents

Description of the Poster and Booklet

MANY TEACHERS AND COMMENTATORS have used visual images to portray disparities in the distribution of income in the United States. The purpose of this poster and booklet is to show, in an easily accessible way, how various groups in the American population are faring in terms of several social indicators. Much of this information is discussed in the media and in classrooms, but the numbers, percentages, and median figures can be confusing and hard to relate to one another.

The poster is an attempt to overcome this problem by presenting the data in a single visual picture. In this form, the relationship of income, wealth, and education to such variables as race, gender, and household type are visible at a glance.

One of the original purposes of the poster was to show the vast differences in incomes across the American population in 1979. Compared with earlier editions, especially with that first poster, many things have changed. This is the eighth edition, which presents data that reflect 2019 incomes (2020 data were also available but not used because of the economic disruption of the COVID pandemic). Inequality in 2019 is substantially greater than it was forty years ago, making the 1979 distribution look much fairer.

The eighth edition is based on the same categories with the one exception of the 2014 poster, which used educational attainment in place of occupation. Given that all the data come from various years of the Annual Socioeconomic Supplement of the March Current Population Surveys (CPS), it is easy to show how family types, races, educational attainment, occupations, and incomes have changed over time because the Census Bureau has contracted the Minnesota Population Center to "harmonize" the answers of different census surveys and for different years of each survey. The data for this poster come from the March 2020 Current Population Survey (CPS); the demographics come from March 2020, but the income and earnings are based on 2019 levels.

In addition, other changes include the rising shares of Hispanics and Asians, a huge increase in the share of workers with a four-year degree (see Figure 4), and an economy in which manufacturing has a much smaller influence. All these changes are documented, and the poster shows how they affect rising inequality. Furthermore, data from 1999 will show whether these changes were occurring in the twenty years since the first edition of this poster/book in 1979 or in the next twenty years from 1999 to 2019.

The icons are distributed along two separate income lines. The graph with larger icons, on the left side of the poster, shows the 91 percent of the population with combined gross household income (before taxes are deducted) up to $280,000. The graph on the right side of the poster depicts the population with incomes of up to the four icons that have incomes over $800,000. Also included with this graph are rows of green dollars to show the average level of wealth of households at

Table 1

Number of icons on the poster broken out by family type

	Married/ cohabitors	Single men	Single women	Single males with dependents	Single females with dependents
1979	756	72	94	13	65
1999	673	117	124	25	62
2019	690	102	116	27	65

different levels of income. Wealth consists of assets held rather than wages and salaries. Most people's wealth consists of tangible things—houses, cars, consumer durables, and so on—while the bulk of the richest people's wealth is composed of financial assets, such as stocks, bonds, insurance policies, and the businesses they own.

THE TABLES AND FIGURES in this booklet complement the poster by presenting a complete mathematical breakdown of each of the statistical relationships. These are the building blocks from which the poster has been constructed.

After all the data are represented, attention is paid to the widely used concept of middle class. In the first booklet, I wrote that the term "middle class" was useless because it was so broad as to have no meaning. This position has been validated in many surveys by the Pew Research Center that show that approximately 90 percent of Americans choose middle class when given the choice of identifying as lower, middle, or upper class. In the second version of the poster,

I reported that the middle class had shrunk between 1979 and 1983.

The poster and accompanying data allow the viewer to investigate what various components of the middle class have in common and the ways in which they differ. The purpose is to stimulate discussion about these important questions rather than provide "answers." The first chapter discusses statistics, mathematical figures, and government surveys. The next six chapters deal with various relationships: families, education, race, income, and wealth. The following two chapters deal with defining five social groups, with three being lower, middle, and upper middle class. Chapter 8 shows the growth of the upper middle class and the growth of the number qualifying as rich. The ninth chapter looks at multiyear experiences of the five income groups. The final chapter explores the causes of income inequality.

At the end of the text are three appendices. The first appendix presents suggestions for classroom use. The second appendix lists references and government data sources. Finally, the third appendix lists cited and uncited papers by this author.

1

Statistics and Sources

NUMBERS ARE USED CONSTANTLY IN PUB-
lic debate, and they lend a certain air of final-
ity and definitiveness. Many people are not taken
in by this ploy and are suspicious of anyone using
numbers; others retreat in awe. Everyone knows
how confusing it is when something they believe
to be true is "refuted" by someone using statistics.
What are they to do—believe their instinct or their
opponent's argument? Fortunately, they are saved
many times by their belief in the quip "There are
three kinds of lies: lies, damned lies, and statistics."

In frustration, many people shy away from data-
driven arguments and turn to anecdotes. I am sure
that you have heard the one about your friend's
feisty ninety-year-old grandmother who smoked
three packs of cigarettes a day her whole adult life,
drank like a fish, and had a cholesterol level of 500.
And so? This is an example of the little jibes that
people take at experts and of the lack of confidence
in the use of statistics. Just because not every single
smoker dies at sixty does not mean that smoking is
not bad for your health.

This is unfortunate because quantitative analysis can be a powerful tool in presenting and
understanding complicated relationships. Part of
the problem is "mathphobia." But it is also true
that statistics can be manipulated. For instance,
a demographic statistic is usually presented as "x
percent of the y population fits the relevant cri-
teria." Whoever defines x and y has tremendous
power over the impression created by that data.

Let us look at a few examples to highlight this
point. A television commercial proclaims that
two-thirds of TV engineers prefer TVs made by
Brand A, while a competing commercial assures
us that two-thirds of TV engineers own Brand B
TVs. These assertions can both be true because
they address different questions—preference and
ownership. Company B may be a broadcasting
company that produces TVs and sells them to its
engineers at a deep discount; so, these engineers
may own brand B but prefer another. Another simple explanation may be that Brand B is cheaper.

Another more complex example involves making international comparisons. In 2000, I spent a
couple of months in Strasbourg, France, while a
friend was spending a month in Paris. He thought
that the quality of life was higher in France than
in America for middle-class families. He reasoned
that the quality of goods was higher (the beloved
corner bakery shop), no one had to worry about
health insurance, the public transportation system was much better, there were more interesting
places to visit, the workweek was shorter, and the
workers took longer vacations.

I argued that there was no way to compare
the two countries because they had different pri-
orities. Yes, the French worked fewer hours, but
this meant that shops were closed from noon on
Saturday through Monday morning. Yes, public
transportation was better, but the roads in the cities were very narrow and hard to navigate. Most
of France was a tourist destination. It was fun to
visit and take in the sights. But a lot of apartment

buildings did not have elevators; having more than one bathroom per apartment was a rarity; and the average living space was a little more than half the size of a typical American house.

When comparing living conditions in Western Europe to those in the United States, many researchers say it is better to be rich in America (because of the very high taxes on wealthy people in Europe) and poor in Europe (because of the extensive social safety net). No one really knows how to accurately compare the living conditions of those in the middle.

My own take on the comparison is that one can't make it. I feel that if you plopped some American suburbanites in the outskirts of Strasbourg, they would feel uncomfortable and miss much of their American life. Conversely, members of the French middle class moving to America would also experience their share of culture shock. The bottom line is that these two societies have high standards of living and choose to live quite differently. To the degree that someone has tried to quantify living standards, the Organization for Economic Cooperation and Development (OECD) reports that in terms of "purchasing power parity," Americans have a significantly higher standard of living.

Statistical Measures

Often, a single number is used to represent the conditions of a group; for example, the typical administrative assistant makes *x* dollars. Clearly some make less and others earn more, but we use a single number to represent all administrative assistants. There are various ways of communicating what is "typical." The average, or mean, salary is determined by adding the salaries of all administrative assistants and dividing by the number of administrative assistants. The median salary, by contrast, is derived by ranking all administrative assistants in order of their income and finding the salary at which half the administrative assistants

make more and half make less. In other words, the median value tells you the salary of the one in the middle. In general, the average tends to be higher than the median because the values at the high end of the distribution raise the mean but do not affect the median.

The mean and median are measures of central tendency—that is, they are different ways of describing the most common feature of a population. Sometimes, however, it is useful to obtain a more complete picture by looking at the status of people who are at different points along the pay scale—for example, the poorest 20 percent or the richest 5 percent. In order to do this, all observations must be ranked according to the appropriate measure. One example that many students are familiar with is their SAT scores. These are reported as a raw score for each test (e.g., 650) and a percentile level (88th percentile). The percentile score reveals how you performed relative to everyone else taking the exam. Often, when reporting about income distribution, analysts divide the population into five groups, or quintiles, and report the average income of each. This convention is used to more fully describe a diverse population.

A population is often divided into different groups or subpopulations. Race and occupation are two factors used in constructing the poster. Each group (e.g., African Americans or farmers) is reported as a percentage of the whole. More detailed analysis separates these into even smaller units, which are reported as percentages of the subpopulation. Given that a family has many characteristics—income, occupation, race, and the number, gender, and age of its members, among others—a variety of information can be reported about it. Each value refers it in a different way to various segments of the overall population with which it shares something in common.

———

Data Sources

Social science statistics come from a variety of sources, with the most common source being surveys of 20,000 to 150,000 respondents. This may surprise many people who think that there are massive data sets with information of all kinds about most people. After all, there are credit agency reports, tax records, Social Security account information, medical records, marriage licenses, and myriad other collections of information about us. Put them all together and you should be able to know most everything about everyone.

Fortunately, this is not the case! Most government agencies have strong protections about using their data for purposes other than what is necessary to perform their function. These data cannot be shared, and they are not linked with one another in a master data set. Marketers, on the other hand, have created synthetic data sets that combine information from many sources for many adults in the country. Social scientists rely on specialized surveys. For example, the official U.S. unemployment rate is announced on the first Friday of every month. A common misperception is that this figure is based on a count of people receiving unemployment compensation checks. This is not the case; the unemployed include all those who are seeking a job, rather than just those who are getting benefits (in fact, less than 40 percent of the unemployed receive benefits). Instead, the unemployment rate is derived from a monthly survey of 80,000 adults.

The long form of the decennial census is an excellent source of information, but it is collected only once every ten years. To provide more timely information, the U.S. government started the monthly Current Population Survey (CPS) in 1964 (replacing a shorter survey that had been started in 1948). Most of the articles you read about earnings, employment, and family status use this survey and its various monthly supplements.

The American government has been an international leader in recognizing the importance of publicly available, accurate information. In addition to the CPS, in 2003 the Census Bureau began conducting the American Community Survey to provide current social information at the state and community levels. There are also many specialized surveys that deal with health, education, and employer practices.

Surveys are widely used because researchers have become confident in their ability to collect limited data that reflects the conditions of the entire population. Sampling statisticians have developed techniques to construct samples that are both cost-efficient and accurate. Some researchers have such confidence in this approach that they suggested that surveys would have provided a better estimate of inner-city populations for the 2000 Census than direct counts.

This counterintuitive proposal appalled many people who felt that a real count had to be better than a limited count. In general, this principle is true, but what about conditions in which you can't get a real count? Virtually everyone involved in conducting past censuses agreed that it was hard to reach all inner-city residents, a historically undercounted population. The choice was not really between a census and a survey but between two imperfect ways of estimating a figure when people were often not available to be counted. Statisticians argued that you could target your resources to get a few counts right and then use the data obtained from this limited, high-intensity census to estimate the populations in many other cities. Not surprisingly, the statisticians lost. The politicians and public did not have as much confidence in survey techniques as they did.

One last thing about surveys needs to be noted. Most surveys are taken at a single point in time and ask about current conditions and income or earnings over the past year. These cross-sectional or snapshot surveys are more useful in describing the state of the overall economy than they are in describing individual conditions. The reason for this is that people's conditions change over time—in particular, the life-cycle effect of school, entry-level jobs, career and advancement, and retirement.

In fact, not all issues of mobility and opportunity can be addressed with cross-sectional surveys. As an alternative, longitudinal or panel surveys follow the same people over many years. Keeping in contact with these people is a huge undertaking and makes longitudinal surveys much more expensive than single-shot surveys. Therefore, they tend to be smaller and there are fewer of them. But they will be cited in this booklet because of the richness of the data that they provide.

2

Family Types

THE POSTER IS BASED ON AN UNUSUAL REPRE-
sentation of families. First, married couples
are represented by separate icons of wives and
husbands with the combined incomes of all family members. Second, cohabitors are treated as a
married couple with shared joint incomes. Third,
single people without dependents are defined as a
family of one and all roommates are separate families of one with their own personal income, race,
and occupation. Four, there are male and female
single parents with children but no spouse.

The poster has 1,000 icons representing people
who are either a family head or spouse. Each icon
shows gender, family status, one of four races/eth-
nicities (Hispanics of all races, whites, blacks, and
Asians—each of these categories are a social and
not a biological group), and one of eight working
statuses (six occupations, retirees, and those not
working but not retired).

Further, each icon is placed on the poster in one
of ten income categories that range from less than
$37,000 to over $800,000. On the poster, there
are two income lines. The large icons on the left
side of the poster represent the 91 percent of icons
with incomes of $0–$280,000. The right side has
the entire income range and smaller icons for those
having incomes above $280,000.

There are over 3,000 combinations of these categories, meaning that 1,000 icons cannot fully represent 200 million adults. The distributions of all
the categories are based on 100,000 cases from the
March 2020 supplement of the monthly Current

Population Survey weighted to accurately represent its share of our population. The exact five ele-
ments of each icon will rarely have 200,000 cases
or a multiple of 200,000 cases. This means there
are many "partial cells" because the poster only
deals with full icons. Thus, the key element in cre-
ating the poster is making sure that all the major
aggregates are correct.

Because only adults who are responsible for
their own well-being are included, 20 percent of
adults are excluded: children over seventeen years
of age who are still living with their parents, and
other relatives of the primary adult or of their
partner—e.g., siblings, elderly parents, or grand-
parents. Roommates are considered two separate
one-person families, but cohabitors are treated
as married. Consequently, 40 percent of the population is not represented on the poster, mainly
because 31 percent of Americans are children living with their parents or another relative—e.g.,
a grandparent. Most but not all (68 percent) are
less than eighteen years old; another 23 percent
are eighteen to twenty-nine, leaving 9 percent
at thirty or older. Another 5 percent are adults
who are relatives of the household head—e.g., a
sibling or parent—and 1 percent are nonrelated
boarders.

Finally, there are three small groups of adults
who have characteristics that are not presented in
the poster because they are too few to reflect five
family types, four races, eight occupations, and ten
income groups. The groups that don't fit are:

FIGURE 1

**Rise of single
adult families by
number of icons:
1979, 1999, 2019**

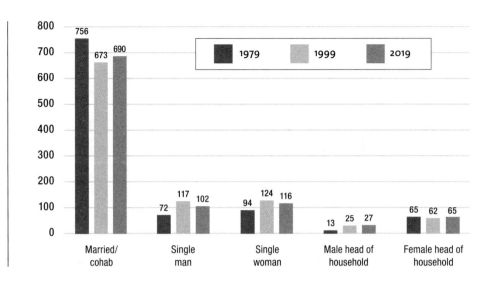

* the 1.5 percent of couples who are of the same sex
* the 2 percent of people who say they are multiracial
* the 4 percent of couples who are of different race/ethnicity; while this is a large group, there are sixteen different combinations of the mixed types, and only two that have more than 1 percent.

The median incomes of same-sex couples and cohabitors are higher than those of straight people (6 percent higher for married people and 21 percent higher among cohabitors). In contrast, the median incomes of biracial couples are 7 percent lower than those who are of the same race. Finally, those who identify as multiracial have median incomes equal to those of Hispanic and higher than those of blacks.

Another group of adults are not represented because they don't live in a private home—e.g., people in institutions such as military barracks, prisons, and mental hospitals. Finally, there are three types of people who have unique features but aren't numerous enough to be adequately represented on the poster; this includes same-sex couples, biracial couples, and those that say that they are multiracial or are members of small racial groups—e.g., Native Americans and Pacific Islanders.

Figure 1 presents the breakdown by family type

of the 1,000 icons on the posters in 1979, 1999, and 2019. The independent adult population consists of husbands, wives, single men, single women, or single men or women with dependents but no spouse—called male- and female-headed households. As noted earlier, cohabitors are treated as married and single people and roommates are each treated as a family of one.

In relation to the 1979 poster, the 1999 poster had 83 fewer icons of married couples. Most of the gains were in the share of single people without families. Today single young adulthood apart from one's family is considered a normal, even cherished, stage in one's life. The other large group of singles is the elderly (primarily women) who have chosen independence, often in retirement communities, over living with adult children. By contrast, in Japan over half of elderly widows live with their children. As a result of these changes, the United States has one of the highest levels of single-person households in the world.

Moving from 1999 to 2019, there was a small increase in the share of married couples. Oddly, the number of female-headed households was the same in all three years, while the number of single fathers doubled in size, but off a very low base. It is interesting to note that female-headed families were not that uncommon in the 1940s and 1950s. Of white families in 1940, 8 percent were headed by women without a spouse present. Today, that

Table 2
Family type by age: 2019, 1979

	Married	Single male	Single female	Male head of household	Female head of household
AGE 2019					
18–29	53%	18%	15%	5%	8%
to 49	76%	8%	6%	3%	8%
64	72%	10%	10%	3%	6%
65 +	63%	11%	20%	2%	5%
AGE 1979					
18–29	72%	12%	9%	1%	6%
to 49	83%	5%	3%	1%	8%
64	80%	4%	8%	1%	7%
65 +	59%	7%	27%	1%	6%

2019 source: Author's computation from 1980, 2000, and 2020 March Supplments of CPS

1979 source: Author's computation from 1980 and 2020 March Supplements of CPS

figure is 12 percent. The change is much more dramatic among black families. In 1940, 16 percent of black families were headed by a female; today 42 percent are. Another important aspect of this change is the increasing proportion who were never married. In the past, single-female-headed households were often caused by a husband's death or abandonment. Finally, it should be noted that women represent 58 percent of single adult households. This reflects the following: (1) women are far more likely to be single parents; (2) women live longer than men, with single elderly women outnumbering comparable men by a three-to-one margin; and (3) many more men than women are in the armed forces or in prisons, and therefore excluded from the data.

Despite this shift to single adult households, nearly 70 percent of nondependent adults live in intact husband-wife couples (including cohabitors). The media give so much attention to divorce and nontraditional living arrangements that most

people expect this number to be much lower. In fact, most single women are elderly widows, while young adults tend to remain single and living away from their parents for only a few years before finding a mate. Divorce has become much more common but, in most cases, is followed by remarriage, in a kind of serial monogamy. The result is often a "blended family," in which children may live with stepparents, half siblings, and stepsiblings.

Some of the decline of married couples is due to demographic changes and big declines in marriage by age. Table 2 shows the division of the five family types based on various age ranges in 1979 and 2019. The share of eighteen- to twenty-nine-year-olds who are married went from 72 percent in 1979 to 50 percent in 2019. Delaying marriage has reflected the cultural change of taking on family obligations in one's twenties. Those who were thirty to sixty-four went from 80 percent married in 1979 to 70 percent in 2019.

3
Race / Ethnicity

THE RACE/ETHNICITY OF THE POPULATION represented by each icon is shown in Table 8. It is important to note that the definition of race is not clear-cut. Many whites have some black, Native American, or Asian ancestors. Hispanics[1] come from many different countries and are mixtures of different races. Studies of African Americans, for instance, reveal that well over half have some European or "white American" ancestry. Finally, there are people who identify as biracial and there are many people who come from small racial groups—e.g., Native Americans, Samoans, and other Pacific Islanders.

Figure 2 shows the remarkable 20 percent decline of non-Hispanic whites over forty years—from 84 percent to 64 percent. The share of blacks was steady at around 10 percent, while the Hispanic share grew by 12 percent. The Hispanic growth made it the dominant nonwhite group: In 1979, blacks were 9 percent versus 5 percent for Hispanics. The positions reversed by 2019 with Hispanics at 17 percent versus blacks at 10 percent. Until 2014, the fourth major race category was "other races." The number of Asians (a combination of many countries) grew tremendously to 7 percent in 2019, and a reasonable estimate is that Asians were half of those "other races" category in the earlier years.

Going forward, it is expected that the number of nonwhites (including white Hispanics) will continue to increase and become a majority at some point in the next several decades. These populations are younger, and their birthrates are slightly higher than that of whites. The explosion of nonwhite students has occurred while the birthrates of these populations have been falling.[2] Contrary to widespread belief, the fall in birthrates has been greatest among teenage girls, especially African Americans. In 1960, the birthrate per 1,000 women 15 to 19 years old was 158 children for African Americans and 79 for whites. In 2010, teenage non-Hispanic whites had 24 births per 1,000 while African Americans and Hispanics had rates of 52 and 56 per 1,000. One of the main reasons for this decline is that young people are marrying and having children later. This means that most teen births now occur out of wedlock (89 percent of blacks and 39 percent of whites) with all the accompanying problems that result.

In addition, we have an inflow of immigrants who are predominantly nonwhite. Among them are many highly educated immigrants who come for college and graduate school and then stay on and become American citizens.

In many elementary and high school districts in

---

1. Government reports often refer to this group as "being of Hispanic origin" and include people of European descent. The vast majority of this category was born in, or can be traced back to, Central or South America.

2. This reduction in family size is common to all the advanced industrial countries; indeed, several European countries and Japan have had negative population growth over the last decade because the number of deaths is outstripping the number of births.

FIGURE 2

Changing
racial
composition:
1979, 1999, 2019

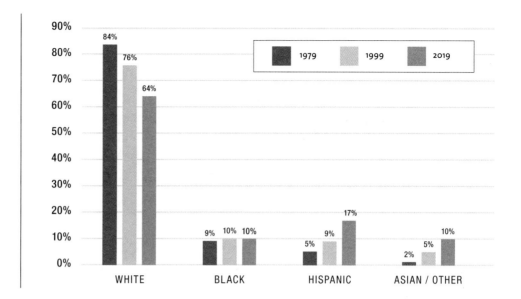

Source: Author's computation
from 1980, 2000, and 2020
March Supplments of CPS

our large metropolitan areas, over half the student body is nonwhite of various backgrounds. It is not unusual for some school districts to have student populations representing over fifty different languages spoken at home.

Figure 3 shows that the share of whites in different age-groups rises dramatically in older age-groups; in 2019, whites make up 50 percent of those under eighteen but 76 percent of those sixty-five and older. This contrasts with the 1979 dominance of whites, ranging from 74 percent of those under eighteen to 88 percent of those sixty-five and older.

For blacks and Hispanics (but not Asians), the pattern is reversed, as the highest concentration is in the youngest age-group and the lowest concentrations are in the older age-groups. Hispanics, however, have a much higher concentration than blacks in the under-eighteen group—26 and 14 percent respectively. The combination of the relatively high concentrations of Hispanics and blacks in the younger age-groups with continuing immigration of Hispanics and Asians will lead to a continuing fall in the white share of our population. One thing that may lessen this effect might be the changing self-identification of many Hispanics to "white" when answering the race question on census surveys.

FIGURE 3

Race
distribution
by age:
2019

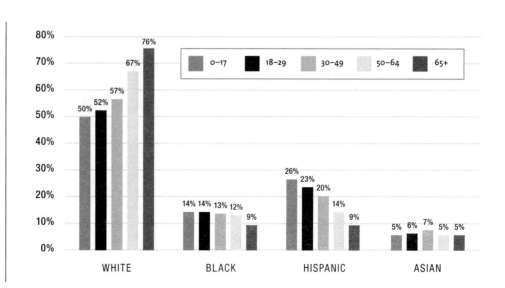

Source: Author's
computation from 2020
March Supplements of CPS

4
Education

THERE ARE MANY REASONS FOR SUPPORT-ing increased educational attainment. For some, education encourages better behavior and more personal satisfaction—higher rates of marriage, less smoking, more healthy practices, and more civic engagement. For others, especially businesses, more-educated workers are better workers. This has become more and more important as the production process has become more complex.

Most important, in today's world, education is used as the primary preparation for work. Those with more education are funneled into the highest-paying jobs. As Figure 4 shows, lifetime earnings rise with more education. While the median life-time earnings of those with a high school diploma and no postsecondary education are $1.6 million (or $40,000 a year over forty years), those with a bachelor's degree earn $1.2 million more. Doctoral

and professional degrees average over $80,000 a year over forty years, leading to considerably more than $3 million in lifetime earnings over a career. Many people compute the "college earnings premium" as 2.8 million divided by 1.6 million and get 175 percent. But this is an understatement because one-third of four-year college graduates get a graduate degree. Therefore, the median lifetime earnings of all BA graduates, including those who get a higher degree, would be $400,000 more, meaning that the college premium is close to 200 percent. Another reason that the premium is higher concerns a series of occupations—clergy, teachers, and employees of nonprofit service organizations—that have relatively low earnings and nonpecuniary rewards.

On the other hand, the premium may be overstated because the most educated may have innate talent. This is an example of selection bias rather

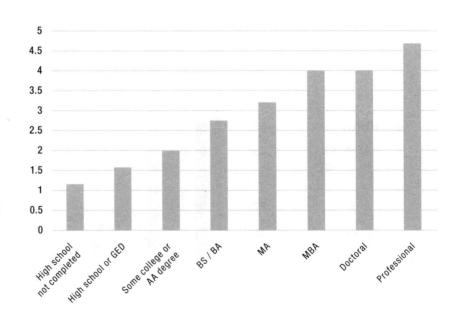

FIGURE 4

Lifetime earnings
by educational
attainment,
in millions of dollars

Source: Georgetown
University Center on
Education and the Workforce
analysis of the US Census
Bureau, American Community
Survey (ACS), 2009–2019.

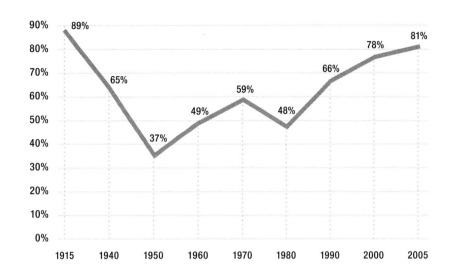

FIGURE 5

College
earnings
premium:
1915–2005

than a return on education. Further, others argue that what we learn in college is not remembered nor useful and that employers use the degree as a proxy for abilities.

My take is based on four premises:

1. While there are some genetic differences, we all start far away from our potential. Children from upper-middle-class and rich parents have many advantages: they are pushed to do well in school, tend to go to schools with more advanced peers, and have access to extra support when needed.

2. In almost all high-income countries, children from age three to eighteen attend pre-K and finish secondary school, and over 60 percent go on to multiple years of two- or four-year colleges.

3. Nearly half of college graduates learn specific skills that help them in their careers—e.g., majors in business, science, IT, and education. All four-year students, however, spend four years figuring out how to satisfy multiple professors' requirements, employing different skills.

4. Historically, the education wage premium has risen and fallen depending on the complex interaction between supply and demand.[3] In *The Race Between Education and Technological Change*, Harvard economists Claudia Goldin and Lawrence Katz track the added earnings that college-educated workers have over those with just a high school education (Figure 6).

When the baby boomers first started finishing their education by going to college in record numbers, there were some indicators that perhaps we had gone too far and produced too many college graduates (see Richard Freeman's 1978 *The Over-educated American*). As we will show in the next chapter, this fear turned out to be unfounded as the earnings of workers with a bachelor's degree relative to workers with only a high school diploma skyrocketed.

Many view the rise in educational attainment as a simple reflection of an age of fast and accelerating technological change, particularly the rise of computers. This is a false view, as technological change has been persistent over the last 200 years.

3. We would have liked to have tracked the associate's/high school degree and bachelor's/associate's degree wage ratios, but information about those getting an associate's degree (as distinct from some college without a degree) only became available in the Current Population Survey in 1992, by which time most of the increase in earnings inequality had occurred.

Table 3
Educational distribution within income levels

Income Group	High school not completed	High school or GED	Some college or AA degree	Bachelor's degree	Graduate degree
Less than $37,000	18%	37%	27%	13%	5%
$37,000 to less than $74,000	10%	32%	30%	20%	9%
$74,000 to less than $111,000	5%	26%	29%	26%	14%
$111,000 to less than $148,000	3%	21%	27%	31%	18%
$148,000 to less than $185,000	2%	16%	23%	35%	24%
$185,000 to less than $222,000	1%	13%	21%	36%	29%
More than $222,000	76%	8%	6%	3%	8%

Source: Author's computation from 2020 March Supplements of CPS

Education is represented on the poster on the inserts at the top of each of the six income groups on the large icon income ladder. Above the sixth insert, there is an insert showing the educational distribution of all those with incomes greater than $222,000. Table 3 shows the distribution of educational attainment in each income group. For all independent adults, the educational breakdown is 8 percent without a high school diploma, 26 percent with a high school diploma or GED, 27 percent with some college or an associate degree, 24 percent with a four-year degree, and 15 percent with a graduate degree (primarily master's degrees).

As this table shows, those in higher income groups have higher numbers of those with a college degree and much lower numbers with those with a high school diploma or less. Comparing the education attainment of those in the lowest income group (less than $37,000) versus those in the highest income group ($222,000 and higher) shows a huge difference. While there are 18 percent of the lowest group who did not finish high school, only 1 percent in the highest group failed to finish high school. Among those with a high school diploma or GED and no college, 37 percent of the low-income

group had this attainment versus 13 percent of the high-income people.

At the other end of education ladder, 29 percent of the high-income group had a graduate degree while only 5 percent of low-income people reached this level (probably mostly still students). Similarly, the high-income group had many more with a four-year degree versus the low-income group—36 to 13 percent.

There is also a big difference in education with respect to people of different races/ethnicity. As Table 4 shows, 41 percent of whites in 2019 had a four-year or graduate degree as their highest attainment, while another 27 percent had some college or a two-year degree. This is a huge jump from 1979, when 19 percent had a four-year or graduate degree as their highest attainment and 15 percent had some college or a two-year degree. In other words, attending college went from 33 to 68 percent over these years.

The educational attainment of Asians in 2019 (no separate data for 1979) is much higher, with 29 percent having a graduate degree. Combining this with 34 percent who have a four-year degree means that 63 percent had at least a BA. This translates into an astonishing 82 percent of Asians

Table 4
Educational attainment by race: 2019, 1979

	High school not completed	High school or GED	Some college or AA degree	Bachelor's degree	Graduate degree
2019					
White	5%	27%	27%	25%	16%
Black	10%	32%	29%	19%	10%
Hispanic	25%	31%	23%	14%	7%
Asian	8%	16%	13%	34%	29%
1979					
White	28%	38%	15%	11%	8%
Black	48%	31%	13%	5%	3%
Hispanic	56%	27%	10%	4%	3%

Table 5
Similar levels of education of husbands and wives: 2019

	WIFE'S EDUCATION				
	High school dropouts	High school or GED	Some college or AA degree	Bachelor's degree	Graduate degree
HUSBAND'S EDUCATION					
High school dropouts	51%	29%	14%	4%	2%
High school or GED	7%	49%	26%	13%	5%
Some college or AA degree	3%	23%	44%	22%	9%
Bachelor's degree	1%	10%	20%	48%	21%
Graduate degree	1%	5%	14%	34%	46%

Source: Author's computation from 2020 March Supplement of CPS

who attend college have at least a BA; the comparable number for whites was 60 percent.

The numbers for blacks may surprise many people because they have heard that only half of the students of many inner-city high schools graduate. This obscures the fact that African American children have made huge strides in closing the racial gap in high school graduation. In 1979, only 8 percent had at least a four-year degree; by 2019, this share grew to 29 percent. At the other end of the education spectrum, 48 percent of blacks in 1979 hadn't finished high school. By 2019 this share dropped to 10 percent. While this number is biased down because the high number of blacks in prison aren't counted, it still is a remarkable educational upgrade.

Finally, many Hispanics in 2019 are recent migrants from Mexico and Central America. One in four did not finish a high school diploma and only 21 percent had an undergraduate or graduate degree. The children of immigrants and their children (third generation) have educational profiles closer to that of African Americans.

The income inequality driven by educational differences is magnified by "assortive mating"—people of similar educational backgrounds marrying each other. The diagonal on Table 5 shows that in nearly 50 percent of all couples in 2019, both members had the same educational attainment. When the husband had a BA degree, 69 percent of wives had a college degree; if the husband had a graduate degree, 80 percent of wives had a college degree. The comparable figures for wives in 1979 were 38 percent if their husbands had a BA and 54 percent if their husbands had a graduate degree.

5
Labor Force Status and Occupations

THE COLORS ON THE ICONS REPRESENT OCCU-
pation or employment status if not in the labor
force. To make the poster representative and under-
standable, the number of categories is limited to
eight: six occupation groups and the nonworking
divided into retired and all others—unemployed,
keeping house, staying at home, on welfare, or dis-
abled (the homeless aren't surveyed). The share of
the employed is less than 50 percent (30 percent are
children). Of adults, 80 percent are responsible or
co-responsible for themselves and for dependents;
of this group, a little more than one-third aren't
employed.

The six occupational categories are: (1) manag-
ers/doctors/lawyers; (2) professionals in business,
education, and health care; (3) clerical workers
and technicians; (4) supervisors, technicians, and
skilled blue-collar workers; (5) less skilled blue-
collar, sales, and service workers; and (6) farmers
and farm laborers. The first two categories have
the highest pay and consist mainly of those with a
four-year or graduate degree. The next two categories are mid-skilled jobs with the first one being
predominantly male workers while the second one
is predominantly female workers. The fifth category has many low-paid manual, retail, and personal and food service workers. The farm category
is very small and is included because of its historic
significance.

It should be noted that the data represented by
the icons do not cover the entire labor force. In particular, many young people living with their parents (or living in dorms) are employed, although
rarely in managerial and professional jobs.

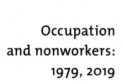

FIGURE 6

Occupation
and nonworkers:
1979, 2019

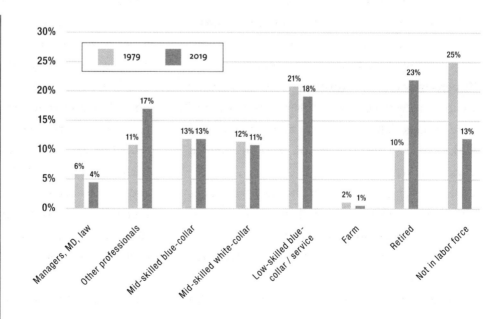

Source: Author's
computation from
1980 and 2020 March
Supplements of CPS

FIGURE 7

Women's
changes:
1979, 2019

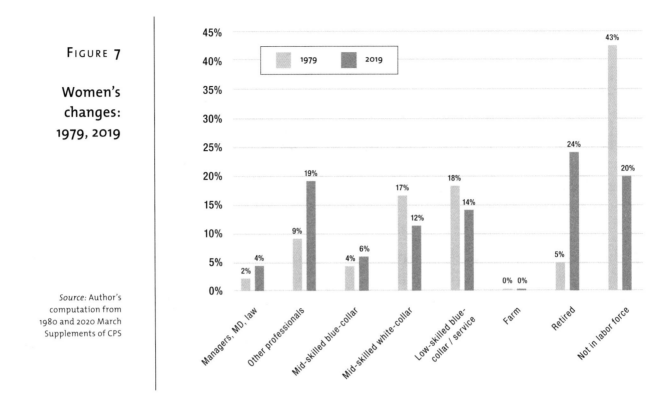

Source: Author's
computation from
1980 and 2020 March
Supplements of CPS

Figure 6 shows the changes in each of the eight categories. Among the employed, the big movements from 1979 to 2019 were the nearly 6 percent point gain in the "other professionals" category and the 3 percent loss in the low-skilled blue-collar, service, and retail job category.

In both 1979 and 2019, women made up 53 percent of all independent adults, but what they did has changed. The greatest difference involved nonworking women: In 1979, 5 percent were retired and 43 percent were out of the labor force, primarily as "homemakers." By 2019, as Figure 7 shows, 24 percent of these women were retired and only 20 percent were not working. In terms of their occupations when employed, there was a swing to more managerial, professional, and self-employed work and less clerical, retail, and low-skilled service and retail work.

Unsurprisingly, education strongly correlates with their occupational attainment. On the most basic level, education affects whether one is working or not. For those who did not complete high school, more than half (54 percent) were not employed, while for men and women with a high school diploma or GED the nonworking share was 43 percent. The nonworking share of the some-college group was 36 percent, and those with a BA or graduate degree had the lowest nonworking shares of 27 and 26 percent.

For those working in a nonagricultural job, there are two ways to show the effects of education on occupation: the shares of occupations by educational level and the educational breakdown by occupation. Panel 1 of Table 6 shows that only those with graduate degrees have a high probability of being employed as managers or professionals. In contrast, only half of those with a four-year degree are employed in these jobs, while those with no college attendance rarely are employed as professionals: 3 percent of those who didn't finish high school or earned a GED and 10 percent of those with a high school diploma or GED. At the other end of the occupation spectrum, 66 percent of high school dropouts were in low-skilled jobs. For those with a high school diploma or GED, 47 percent were in these jobs while the comparable figure for those with some college but not a four-year degree was 32 percent. Of college graduates, only

Table 6
Education and occupations: 2019

Panel 1: Occupations of different education levels

	Managers, MD, law	Other professionals	Mid-skilled blue collar	Mid-skilled white collar	Low-skilled BC/service
High school not completed	1%	2%	24%	6%	66%
High school diploma or GED	2%	8%	27%	17%	47%
Some college or AA degree	3%	17%	24%	23%	32%
Bachelor's degree	7%	43%	19%	17%	15%
Graduate degree	21%	52%	12%	10%	6%

Panel 2: Educational Levels of Occupations

	High school not completed	High school or GED	Some college or AA degree	Bachelor's degree	Graduate degree
Manager, MD, law	1%	5%	13%	29%	52%
Other professionals	0%	6%	17%	43%	33%
Mid-skilled blue collar	6%	29%	30%	24%	10%
Mid-skilled white collar	2%	23%	36%	28%	10%
Low-skilled BC / service	13%	39%	30%	14%	3%

Source: Author's computation from 2020 March Supplement of CPS

6 percent of graduate degree holders were in the lowest occupation group versus 15 percent of those with a four-year degree.

The data in Table 6, Panel 1, do not differ that much from the 1979 situation because better-paying jobs have higher-educated workers. This is deceiving because there was a huge increase in the share of those who have a BA or graduate degree. Panel 2 shows loss of access to the highest-paying jobs for those without at least a BA. In 2019, 81 percent of "managers+" jobs were held by those with a BA or graduate degree. The comparable figure in 1979 was 51 percent. There were openings in top managerial jobs for those who had not attended college, but while 31 percent of managerial jobs were held by those with no college

in 1979, only 6 percent of managerial jobs were held by those who had not attended college in 2019.

The "other professionals" group is diverse and includes teachers at all levels, artists, clergy, social workers, writers, scientists, architects, and many business occupations—e.g., accountants, stockbrokers, sales reps, and human resources managers. While teachers and clergy mostly require a graduate degree, their pay is more like that for middle-skill jobs in contrast to other occupations in this group. Overall, the share of the "other professionals" group that had a graduate or four-year degree grew from 60 percent in 1979 to 78 percent in 2019. Most of that increase was due to more businesspeople having college degrees.

6
Family Incomes

INCOME IS USUALLY REGARDED AS A PROXY FOR one's standard of living and perhaps well-being. Obviously, this does not mean that everyone with a low income is unhappy and everyone with a high income is content. Rather, most people believe that access to more and better goods, houses, and amenities makes life more enjoyable. Higher incomes, then, are preferable and can serve as an indicator of "leading the good life."

The main purpose of the poster is to display income distribution by placing demographic icons in different places on the poster. The large icons are placed on the income line in six groups of $37,000 from $0 to $222,000. The top income was chosen so that approximately 90 percent of the 1,000 icons were on this income line. As Table 7 shows, nearly half of independent adults (484 icons) are in the bottom two income groups. The whole income distribution is presented on the right side of the poster with smaller icons and is topped by the four icons with incomes of $800,000 and more.

Figure 8 shows how income distribution in 2019 compares with the income distribution in 1979 adjusted for inflation. The 2019 incomes are higher and the gap between the two incomes increases with every five percentiles. At the tenth percentile, 2019 incomes are 31 percent greater than 1979 incomes. At the fiftieth percentile they are 43 percent higher. By the seventy-fifth percentile, the gap grows to 65 percent and then reaches 100 percent at the ninety-fifth percentile. The very definition of rising inequality is that income gains over time

are greater as incomes are higher. Clearly, these numbers show rising gains, with particularly large gains at the top of the income ladder.

Figure 8 shows the income distributions of the five family types. As is evident, couples have much higher incomes at all levels of the income ladder. The medians run from $30,000 for single women (mainly elderly widows) to nearly $100,000 for couples. The second-highest incomes are the small number of men with dependents—$68,000 at

Table 7
Number of icons in 10 income groups: 2019

Less than $37,000	231
$37,000 to less than $74,000	253
$74,000 to less than $111,000	184
$111,000 to less than $148,000	115
$148,000 to less than $185,000	77
$185,000 to less than $222,000	47
$222,000 to less than $280,000	39
$280,000 to less than $400,000	32
$400,000 to less than $800,000	17
$800,000 and up	5

Source: Author's computation from 2020 March Supplement of CPS

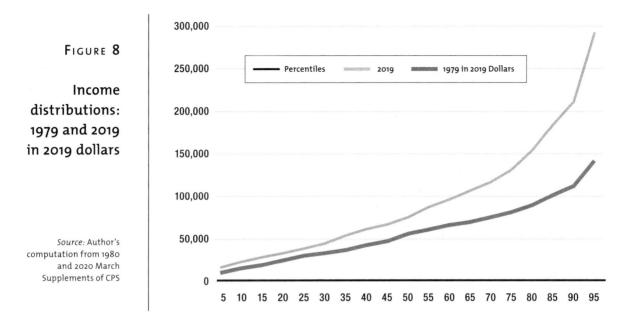

the median. Somewhat surprisingly, women with dependents have higher median incomes than single men—$45,000 and $40,000 respectively. The median income for low-income women with children on welfare is offset by the number of divorced and single mothers who have medium- to well-paying jobs. Similarly, the high pay of young professional males is offset by the many non–college graduates in low- to modest-paying jobs. Since there are 690 icons in couples, the overall median is $76,100—higher than the medians of all noncouple families.

As Table 8 shows, the median income of the 50 percent of couples in which both individuals are working is $127,000. Couples in which only one person is working have a median income just slightly less than the overall median, which includes single-adult families. The incomes of couples in which neither partner is working is relatively low, which is unsurprising as many of them rely on Social Security and have experienced periods of unemployment.

In the case of nearly half of the couples, neither partner has a college degree, and these couples

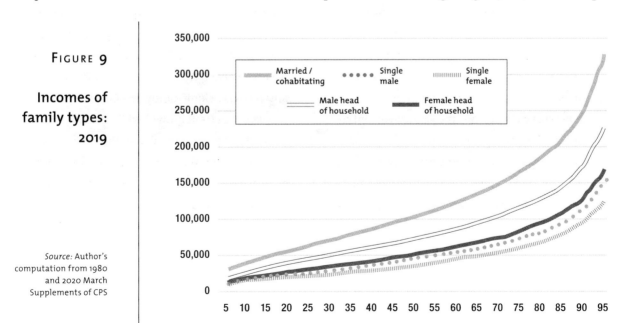

Measuring Inflation

A DOLLAR DOES NOT BUY AS MUCH OVER TIME.
Price inflation—which is the same thing as costing more—is almost always present in advanced industrial countries, the U.S. Federal Reserve Board's target is 2 percent per year. Following the change in a commodity's price over time is difficult because products tend to embody new features and improvements, which requires disentangling the cost of the upgrades from the listed price to calculate the "pure" price change. The U.S. Department of Commerce employs thousands of people to go into stores around the country to monitor prices and evaluate if the quality of a product has improved since the previous year. If so, they estimate how much of the added price is from an improvement in quality rather solely an increase in price. Each month the Department of Commerce releases a report on overall inflation and price changes of many separate commodities.

However, in the past forty years, there have been six major and many small changes in how inflation is computed. Oddly, all the major changes led to higher growth and less inflation.

These changes have led to three separate series of adjusting for inflation. First, the official price series, as found on the Department of Commerce website, uses the year-to-year inflation numbers using the methodology of those years. The CPI-U-RS (RS = research series) is based on applying the 2000 methodology to all years back to 1947. The Bureau of Labor Statistics and Census Bureau use this approach to report historical series in real prices.

In 2002, a joint panel of experts at the Bureau of Labor Statistics and the Census Bureau created a methodology for a new price deflator, the chained consumer price index, or C-CPI, but for the first time, politicians prohibited its use because lower inflation would lead to more people in higher tax brackets [a Republican concern] and a lower annual inflation adjustment to Social Security payments [a Democratic concern].

The Congressional mandate to continue to use the CP-RS was limited to Commerce reports. Other researchers became concerned that the CPI-U-RS was underreporting growth, and they turned to the personal consumption expenditures deflator (PCE) prepared by the Bureau of Economic Analysis of the Commerce Department because it used the chained methodology and went back to 1929.

In a 2017 paper, I posed a simple example to show the differences among the three price deflators. If median income was $25,000 in 1979 and $50,000 in 2014, how much real growth was there using these three price deflators? The answers vary significantly: the CPI-U deflator showed 16 percent growth while the CPI-U-RS showed 31 percent growth and the PCE's growth was 46 percent. While the poster is a snapshot of 2019 data, the PCE deflator is used to convert 1979 dollars into 2019 dollars.

Table 8
Median incomes of couples by number working and number with a college degree

Number working	Share	Median income
0	20%	$55,690
1	30%	$84,400
2	50%	$127,001

Number with a college degree	Share	Median income
0	47%	$70,,002
1	23%	$112,000
2	29%	$152,417

Source: Author's computation from 2020 March Supplement of CPS

---

have a median income slightly less than the overall medians. In contrast, for the 29 percent of couples in which both individuals have a college degree, their median income is over $150,000. One-third of them have incomes over $200,000.

Figure 10 shows the income distributions of the six types of occupations and the two nonworking categories (retired and the combination of various nonworking people). The high pay of the occupation group of managers, medical doctors, and lawyers is the basis of high family income with a median of $180,00 and with nearly 25 percent of them making $300,000 and more. Surprisingly, the incomes of the "other professional" group are slightly higher than those for the two middle-skill groups. While business professionals, engineers, IT workers, and scientists have high salaries, this group also includes lower-paying occupations, such as clergy, teachers, social workers, artists, and writers. From an economist point of view,

FIGURE 10

Income distributions by occupations: 2019

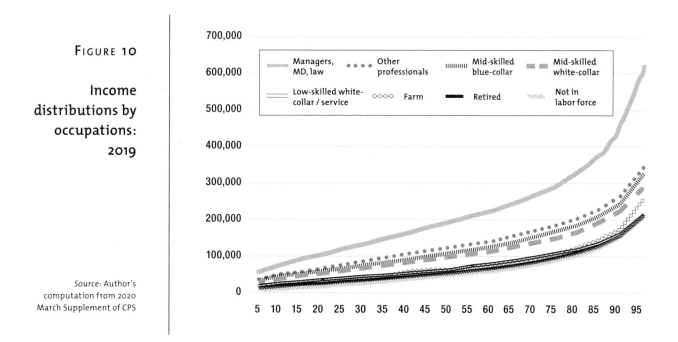

Source: Author's computation from 2020 March Supplement of CPS

FIGURE 11

Income
distributions by
race/Hispanic:
2019

Source: Author's
computation from 2020
March Supplement of CPS

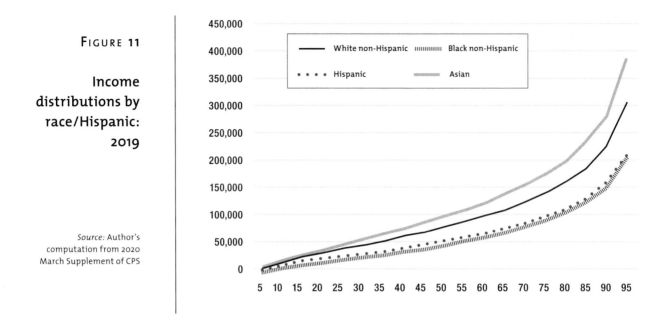

these highly educated people are are not income maximizers.

Finally, there are the four groups that are lower on the income ladder and have somewhat similar distributions. Combined, these groups represent 60 percent of the icons (two-thirds are not employed). Low-end service jobs account for only 10 percent of independent adults.

The final indicator of different incomes is race/ethnicity. Figure 11 shows the income distributions of all Hispanics, whites, blacks, and Asians. The main findings are that whites no longer have the highest incomes and that Hispanics have slightly higher incomes than blacks. Because of the educational attainments that Asians have over whites, especially at the graduate level, the median income of Asians is $102,000 versus $84,000 for whites. The median for Hispanics is $59,000, which is higher than for blacks at $51,000. In 1979, whites had much higher incomes than Hispanics and blacks. The median for Hispanic incomes was 21 percent less than for whites, while the median for blacks was 40 percent lower than for whites. There were no data for Asians in 1979.

7
Wealth

WEALTH IS DIFFERENT FROM INCOME. Income is the amount of money that comes into a household from varying sources during a year. Wealth (sometimes referred to as net worth) is the total monetary value of what a household owns, minus debts. This includes consumer durables such as houses, cars, stereos, the value of owned businesses, and so on, plus financial assets such as stocks, bonds, savings accounts, property, cash value of life insurance policies, and the like.

The biggest asset of many households is the equity value of their homes. Business assets are another.

Table 9 shows wealth by the ten income groups on the poster. Those with incomes below $74,000 have virtually no wealth. With each step up, family wealth increases by about $150,000 for income medians through $185,000. After that, each step is larger until reaching $10 million at the top.

So, who is rich in terms of wealth? One measure would be a guarantee of somewhere near $400,000

Table 9

Median net worth by poster income groups and number of dollar signs assigned to each group on the poster: 2019

Income groups	Median wealth	Number of $ signs shown on poster
Less than $37,000	$0	0
$37,000 to less than $74,000	$14,800	0.3
$74,000 to less than $111,000	$121,000	2.4
$111,000 to less than $148,000	$284,100	5.7
$148,000 to less than $185,000	$407,350	8.1
$185,000 to less than $222,000	$689,100	13.8
$222,000 to less than $280,000	$1,099,200	22
$280,000 to less than $400,000	$1,752,600	35
$400,000 to less than $800,000	$3,811,540	76
$800,000 and up	$10,079,600	202

Source: Author's computation from 2019 Survey of Consumer Finances (SCF)

SOCIAL SECURITY AS WEALTH

IN ESSENCE SOCIAL SECURITY IS A BRILLIANT, complex system of enforced savings that lead to guaranteed incomes after you retire. The cash benefits are guaranteed for life and are increased each year to account for inflation. The system also includes survivorship and disability benefits. Finally, Medicare and Medicaid are companion programs that provide free and subsidized health care for all those over sixty-five.

This is accomplished not by individual accounts but by current workers and their employers paying into the system that pays for current retirees. These payments are the equivalent of individual savings and additional savings of employer's added compensation. Each year the government adds to a personal account of yearly earnings. Eventually, the average of the thirty-five highest inflation-adjusted years of earning is the basis in determining people's yearly benefits. The payout is not proportional but is based on formulas that benefit low earners and give a lower payout ratio for high earners. In other words, high earners subsidize low earners':

* For up to the first $14,00 (rounded to the nearest thousand), the benefit is 90 percent of the adjusted thirty-five year average;

* Between $14,000 to $74,000, the added benefit is increased by 32 percent of the difference between a person's average earnings over $14,000;

* The added difference between $74,000 and $147,000 is only 15 percent of the average earnings over $74,000;

* And earnings over $147,000 are not taxed and don't increase benefits .

Economists believe that if people have guaranteed control of valuable assets over time, it can be "capitalized" to get its value today. Consequently, the value of medical programs and access to disability and survivor benefits is worth several hundreds of thousands of dollars. Similarly, one's lifetime cash payments might run from $200,00 to nearly $1 million. Clearly, people make savings decisions based on their expectations of receiving Social Security and medical benefits, and it makes sense to include the value of these programs as part of their wealth. Several studies do this and obviously get much lower wealth inequality for those over sixty.

for every year without working. Your residence(s) if you're "rich" will almost always be worth several millions. You will have financial assets that average yearly returns of a minimum of 3–4 percent. A net worth of several millions with housing equity doesn't meet these parameters, while $20 million does. Fifteen million might also work if you are not overly extravagant.

As for millionaires, according to the 2019 Survey of Consumer Finances, 11 percent of all families reached this level. For those aged fifty-five to seventy-four, when their household net worth was at its peak, 19 percent were millionaires. Eighty percent of this group had a net worth between $1 million and $5 million. Two percent had between $5 million and $15 million, and 2 percent had over $15 million. For those who were fifty-five to seventy-four and had a college degree, 40 percent were

FIGURE 12

Income
and wealth
by age:
2019

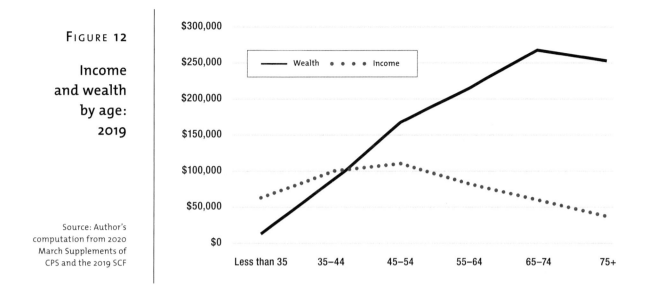

Source: Author's
computation from 2020
March Supplements of
CPS and the 2019 SCF

millionaires, 10 percent had between $1 million and $5 million, another 7 percent had between $5 million and $15 million, leaving 3 percent with more than $15 million.

Except for those who receive a large inheritance, wealth is accrued over a lifetime. As Figure 14 shows, median wealth increases steadily through the age of seventy-four, and the decline in wealth of those above seventy-five isn't that large.

In contrast, median income grows at a much slower rate and begins to decline after age fifty-five. It is much lower for those seventy-five and older. For those who are eighteen to twenty-four and who are no longer living with their parents, median income is $40,700. As people age into their late twenties and early thirties, they start to find their niche. The median income of twenty-five- to thirty-year-olds rises to $72,300. By their late thirties, workers are in their prime earning years. The median income of thirty-five- to forty-four-year-olds is $97,000. People reach their peak income—median at $102,000—between the ages of forty-five and fifty-four. For workers aged fifty-five through sixty-four, their children are often no longer living with them, and they have purchased what

consumer durables they need. Many either retire or reduce the number of hours they work.

Finally, adults over sixty-five have a sharp reduction in cash income, yet, in surveys from the Employee Benefits and Retirement Institute, almost two-thirds of retired people report living as well in retirement as they did in their fifties. This is due to a number of factors: lower expenses because mortgages are often paid off, children are in middle age and independent, and there are no commuting and working expenses; the benefits of more free time; and diminished expectations, in that people adjust to their circumstances.

Going forward, there are concerns that tomorrow's retirees won't have it as good as today's retirees because of the decline of company pensions, now replaced with individual 401(k) and related plans. These plans are better than company pensions for people who change jobs often. Pensions work better for those who stay with the same employer for decades because pensions are based on years of service and the highest pay. Individual retirement accounts shift the investment risk to workers and can be reduced when people take out loans during tough times.

8

The Rise of the Upper Middle Class

THE LINK BETWEEN FAMILY INCOME AND standard of living depends on the number of people that the family must support. For federal relief programs, a multiple of the Federal Poverty Line (FPL) is used, depending on the number of people related to the household head. It does not increase linearly because there are economies of scale. Costs don't increase in proportion to the number of individuals in the household because they can share expenses. While the expression "two can live as cheaply as one" is an exaggeration, providing for two does not cost twice as much in living costs as living alone. Using the most common procedure, size-adjusted incomes are converted to family-of-three-equivalents. For example, $100,000 for a family of three is equivalent to $57,735 for a single person living alone. Or to put it another way, a family of four with an income of $115,470 has the same living standard as a three-person family with an income of $100,000.

Another factor that affects how people feel about their income is how it compares with that of their peers. For those who live in a neighborhood where most family incomes are over $100,000, then an income of $50,000 will seem low. However, in a neighborhood with an average family income of $20,000, this same $50,000 will seem high. An income of $40,000 might support a comfortable standard of living in smaller cities and rural areas but wouldn't go as far in many large cities, where rents and housing costs are high. There are other trade-offs that make simple comparisons of

standard of living difficult—for example, the wide-open spaces and recreational opportunities in the countryside versus the cultural opportunities and excitement of big cities.

MOST AMERICANS consider themselves part of the middle class. For many years, the Pew Research Center has asked people to identify their class, choosing from lower class, lower middle class, middle middle class, upper middle class, and upper class. The results are reasonably consistent, with 90 percent saying middle class (20 percent lower middle class and 20 percent upper middle class), less than 2 percent saying upper class, and 8–10 percent saying lower class.

Many people talk about the conditions of the middle class, but few define it, and the term "upper middle class" is equally ambiguous. Because people tend to live in communities with people with similar incomes, they view themselves as being near the middle because their neighbors' circumstances are like their own even if their incomes are significantly below or above the U.S. median.

The concept of social class knits together multiple factors such as income, wealth, education, prestige, and cultural sophistication, so there is no agreed-upon definition of "middle class." One way to characterize the middle class is by identifying those who clearly are not in it. The rich aren't middle class because they have resources that permit them to have the best of many things. The poor

FIGURE 13

Growing upper
middle class:
1979, 2014, 2019

Source: Author's computation
from 1980, 2015, and 2020
March Supplements of CPS

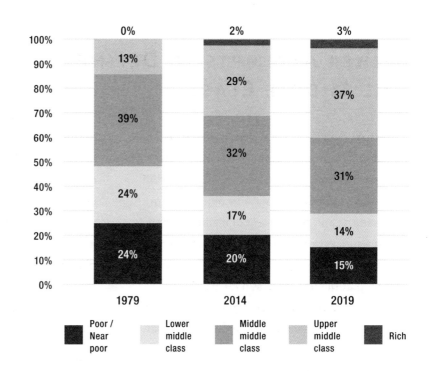

and near-poor have very limited options and often rely on means-tested government programs to meet their living expenses. Because defining by exclusion leaves a very broad middle class, many people divide it into three segments—upper, middle, and lower. But even these divisions cover a broad swath of living standards. Lower-middle-class people generally have modest living standards, while those in the upper middle class have considerably higher living standards than just the basic necessities and have discretionary income available to spend on higher-quality goods and services (e.g., bigger homes, better appliances, eating out, and foreign travel).

Studying the middle class requires an operational definition. I use current income to define class because it is closely related to all the factors associated with social class and because data on current family income are readily available. But families are of different sizes and therefore have different numbers to support. Consequently, there is not one poverty threshold but different thresholds depending on the number of people in the family. Similarly, to determine families' well-being we need to adjust for number of people in the family.

The median income of families of three are closest to the overall median income, so I adjust family incomes to family-of-three equivalents. There is a standard method to do this and is based on families of one or two to have a higher family-of-three equivalents, while families with four or more members have a lower family-of-three equivalents. Specifically, a single person with an income of $57,735 has a family-of-three equivalent of $100,000. Other incomes that are $100,000 family-of three equivalents are $81,650 for a family of two, $115,470 for a family of four, and higher incomes for larger families.

Using the family-of-three approach, I define five classes:

* Poor and Near-Poor: 149 percent of poverty and lower; put in 2019
* Lower Middle Class: between 150 and 249 percent of poverty;
* Middle Middle Class: between 250 and 499 percent of poverty;
* Upper Middle Class: between 500 and 1,749 percent of poverty;
* Rich: above 1,749 percent of poverty.

OTHER ATTEMPTS TO DEFINE THE MIDDLE CLASS

THERE HAVE BEEN AT LEAST TWO OTHER METHOD-
ologies for defining the middle class. The Pew
Research Center and the OECD define the middle
class as including those with incomes that are
between 75 and 200 percent of median income
(At my suggestion, Pew uses family-of-three
income equivalents). Using this approach, they
found that the middle class has shrunk over
time. This approach has two problems: first, the
incomes of their middle class grow substantially; second, more people move up to their richer
group than move down to their lower income
group. One can easily argue that the two pos-
itives outweigh the one negative. In essence,
they show growing prosperity with more inequality.

The Brookings Institution has also given us
a definition of the middle class as those in the
middle three income quintiles each year. Using this methodology, which does not compare
incomes and does not take into account demographics, the size of the middle and upper middle classes never changed, and they don't report
the income growth of their middle class.

The poverty income for a family of three in 2014 (when I first developed this methodology) was about $20,000. As such, the family-of-three equivalent income for the upper middle class ranged from $100,000 to $350,000. This is a useful but crude approach for examining the upper middle class. It would be better to adjust for costs of living in different parts of the country, but these data aren't available. Overall, the approach is sound, as the overestimate of the number of people in the upper middle class in high-cost areas of the country is offset by the underestimate in low-cost areas of the country. The 2019 threshold for an upper-middle-class family of three incomes is just under $107,000; the level for a single person is just under $62,000, while a family of four needs a bit more than $123,0000 to qualify for the upper middle class. The years from 2014 to 2019 saw steady income growth leading to higher incomes across the income ladder. The upper middle class grew from 13 percent in 1979 to 31 percent in 2014 to 37 percent in 2019 (see Figure 12). While the rich went from less than half a percent in 1979 to 3 percent in 2019, the share of families in the other three income classes declined between 1979 and 2019: by 5 percentage points for poor and near-poor, 10 points for lower middle class, and 8 points for middle middle class.

In addition to more families moving into the top two income classes (upper middle class and rich), those classes also have experienced strong income growth over these years, leading to their share of total income growing from 30 percent in 1979 to 61 percent in 2014 to 72 percent in 2019.

The Demographics of the Upper Middle Class and the Rich

There is considerable diversity among the upper middle class and the rich even though certain demographic groups are more likely than others to qualify for this group, with incomes in 2019 of over $109,000. Table 10 shows both the probability that a member of a specific demographic group is in the UMC/R (incidence) as well as the composition

Table 10
Demographics of the upper middle class and rich (UMC/R) by incidence and composition: 2019

	UMC / R incidence	UMC / R share
BY HOUSEHOLD TYPE		
Married couples and cohabitants	48%	81%
Single men	28%	8%
Single women	20%	7%
Male with dependents	27%	2%
Female with dependents	15%	2%
BY RACE/ETHNICITY		
Non-Hispanic white	43%	76%
Non-Hispanic black	23%	7%
Hispanic	22%	8%
Asian	45%	8%
BY EDUCATION		
No high school completion	9%	0%
High school or GED	24%	16%
Some college or AA degree	34%	24%
BA degree	55%	34%
Graduate degree	68%	26%
BY AGE		
19–29	25%	6%
30–49	43%	38%
50–64	48%	36%
65 and older	31%	20%

Source: Author's computation from 2020 March Supplement of CPS

of the UMC/R along demographic lines. I examine incidence and composition by household type, race/ethnicity, educational attainment, and age.

Across household types, individuals in married or cohabiting households have the highest incidence of being in the UMC/R and make up the lion's share of those in the upper classes. For example, 48 percent of couples have incomes that qualify them to be in the UMC/R, and they make up 81 percent of all people in these top income groups. In contrast, 26 percent of single men with or without dependents, 21 percent of single women, and 15 percent of women with dependents are in the UMC/R. None of the noncoupled household types reach even 10 percent of the UMC/R.

In terms of race/ethnicity, UMC/R incidence shows high ratios for white and Asian people (43 and 45 percent respectively) and low values for black and Hispanic people (23 and 22 percent respectively. The vast majority of people (77 percent) in the UMC/R group are non-Hispanic white people. Another 9 percent are of Asian descent, 6 percent are non-Hispanic black people, and 7 percent are Hispanic people. People with higher levels of educational attainment are more likely to be in the UMC/R and compose a larger portion of the group than those with less formal schooling.

With respect to UMC/R incidence, 55 percent of those with a BA make it to the UMC/R and 68 percent of those with a graduate degree reach this income threshold (many highly educated people who don't reach this income level are young or retired). These numbers compare with 34 percent of those with a two-year degree or some college but no postsecondary degree, 24 percent for those who graduated from high school, and 9 percent for those that didn't complete high school. The UMC/R is composed of many people with a four-year or graduate degree, 60 percent in all. Among those individuals in the UMC/R without four-year degrees, many are married to or cohabiting with someone who holds at least a BA. Overall,

74 percent of those in UMC/R either have a college degree or live with someone with a degree.

Finally, UMC/R incidence shows a strong life-cycle pattern as people enter the labor market, find a good job, develop seniority and skills, marry, and then retire. For those under thirty, only 25 percent have family-of-three incomes that put them in UMC/R The ability to reach the UMC/R is at 43 percent for those between ages thirty and forty-nine, while 48 percent of those between fifty and sixty-four reach a plateau. Nearly one in three older people have incomes high enough to be in the UMC/R.

Put another way, the UMC/R is made up predominantly of those between the ages of thirty and sixty-four. Just 6 percent of all individuals in the UMC/R are below age thirty, while 20 percent are sixty-five or older. A lot of attention is properly focused on low-income seniors, but those who did well when younger can combine Social Security and other retirement accounts (pensions or personal IRAs and investments). These are the people who have created the industry of upscale living for fifty-five-and-older active adults with the option of having assisted care when needed.

All these numbers add up to a UMC/R that is mainly married white people between the ages of thirty and sixty-four and in a household with at least one person with a college degree. Focusing on nonelderly couples, Figure 13 shows that 74 percent of families in which both partners have a college degree make it to the UMC/R. If the couple includes one person with a college degree, 58 percent have UMC/R incomes. And for those in which neither person has a college degree, 30 percent have UMC/R incomes—which is below the national average.

As Figure 13 shows, there is a similar gradient depending on the number of workers in the couple. While 68 percent of the incomes of couples in which both people work are higher than the UMC/R threshold, 37 percent of those in which one person works reach this level. Among the

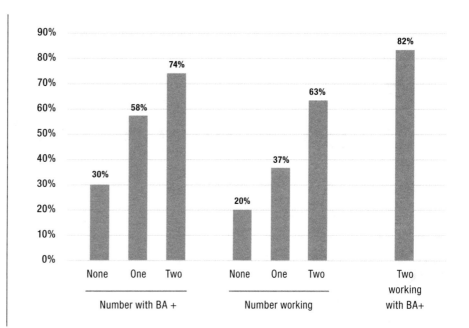

FIGURE 14

Share in
upper middle class
or rich among
non-elderly and
cohabiting couples:
2019

Source: Author's computation from
2020 March Supplements of CPS

small group of nonelderly couples in which neither partner works, 30 percent are in the UMC/R because they either retired young or happened to be not working during the time of the survey. Finally, 82 percent of couples in which both partners have at least BAs and have jobs are in the UMC/R.

We care about trends in family incomes because we think that incomes are a good proxy for standards of living. The Census 2019 income **report** shows a median household income of just under $69,000, although the median for couples is $102,000. Another problem with the census is that it treats both a family of four with two working parents and a single-person household with the same incomes as having the same standard of living. The approach used here adjusts for family size and focuses on "independent adults"—thus a single-person household is one adult while a married couple has two independent adults. As America has more single-adult households, this demographic change lowers the median income.

9
Incomes over Many Years

A CPS SURVEY IS A "CROSS-SECTIONAL" PICture of a single year. The historical comparisons that have been made here and elsewhere are based on "similarly situated people"—in other words, the families at the median in one year are not the same people at the median in respective years (for example, in the many comparisons of 1979 and 2019). In contrast, longitudinal panel surveys follow the same people over many years and sometimes over many decades. We now have many longitudinal studies either run by or paid for by the U.S. government. The first one, the Panel Study on Income Dynamics (PSID), was begun in 1968 by the federal Office of Economic Opportunity and now conducted by the Survey Research Center at the University of Michigan. In 1997, they switched from yearly follow-ups on family composition, earnings, and incomes to biannual surveys.

Researchers who first encounter this longitudinal survey are often surprised by the number of year-to-year changes. Volatility is high at each end of the spectrum. In the PSID, one-third of those in the bottom quintile are there for only one year and experience an average of 80 percent income gain in the following year. The same applies to the top quintile where one-third are there for only one year and have a much lower income in the following year

An example of multiyear results differing on a single-year basis is the poverty rate over the span of five years of varying annual incomes. In my 2010 book *Rebound: Why America Will Emerge Stronger from the Financial Crisis*, I reported that half the people who started in poverty had one or more years of higher incomes that led to their average five-year income—considerably above the poverty threshold. On the other hand, because of periodic bad year fluctuation, the percentage of people who spent at least one year in poverty is 2.5 times higher than the first-year poverty rate; and because volatility is very high for low-income people, only one in four people who started in poverty were in "persistent poverty," meaning at least four out of five years in poverty.

In a 2019 paper ("Life-Cycle Income Trajectories, 1967 to 2016"), I explored volatility and personal income paths. Using size-adjusted income classes, Table 11 is a transition matrix of income groups from 2000 to 2014 for those who were ages twenty-five to forty-four in 2000. For those who were poor and near-poor (PNP) in 2000, 60 percent were still in this income group in 2014 while 40 percent moved up—30 percent to the LMC, 8 percent to the MMC, and even 2 percent to the UMC. Although 18 percent of the LMC moved down, 39 percent moved up to the MMC and 2 percent to the UMC. Only 1 percent of those who started in the MMC fell to the PNP, while 8 percent fell to the LMC. This was offset by 23 percent moving up to the UMC. Finally, only 12 percent moved down to the MMC and 2 percent moved up to the rich group (too few cases started in the rich group in 2000 for this age-group).

Table 11

Income group transitions; income classes in 2014 based on
their income class in 2000

THIRD PERIOD	2014 INCOME CLASS			
2000 Income class	Poor & near-poor	Lower middle class	Middle middle class	Upper middle class
Poor and near-poor	60%	30%	8%	2%
Lower middle class	18%	43%	37%	2%
Middle middle class	1%	8%	68%	23%
Upper middle class	0%	0%	12%	88%

Source: Author's computation from the Panel Study of Income Dynamics

One way to show volatility is to look at the share of the population that had years in which they had family incomes that put them in the UMC. Because the PSID is fielded every other year, there are only eight years of information from 2000 to 2014 for this age-group. Upward volatility led to 60 percent having at least one year of income that put them in the UMC and 48 percent had two or more years with this income. Because of downward volatility, 55 percent of those whose average income qualified as being in the UMC continued to be in the UMC, with incomes in at least seven of those years that put them in the UMC.

10

The Many Causes of Inequality

INCOME INEQUALITY HAS BEEN GROWING since the early 1980s, and this has led many to argue that something must be done. In 2003, an article by Thomas Piketty and Emmanuel Saez used a new data source, income tax records, which showed that the incomes of the bottom half of the income ladder had stagnated. In the following years, as they updated their data, they reported the same results. Many authors, citing these findings, produced books cataloging the problems of American capitalism. In other words, the idea of stagnating middle-class incomes became conventional wisdom.

A small group of critics, including myself, criticized their methodology, and eventually, in 2017, the Piketty team (now including Gabriel Zucman) used a new approach that showed that the change in median real income from 1979 to 2014 had grown by 33 percent in contrast to the minus 8 percent found in their original approach.

Opinion polls have become commonplace, but they need to be looked at closely, especially since many of them have few respondents. For example, one frequently cited figure is the share of Americans who think that the economy isn't doing well—a question that is asked in many polls. But this question is often interpreted as the respondent's general feeling on the state of the country. As such, the cross tabs by political parties show a strong pattern issue: if your party holds the presidency then you tend to answer this question positively; and if your party doesn't hold it, you answer

negatively. Consequently, the last two times there was a change in the party of the presidency, there was a huge swing in the answers to this question. For those whose party lost, there was a big switch from thinking things are going well to saying that things are going badly. For the party that gained the presidency, there was an equal switch from being critical of the current situation to being positive.

The 2019–2020 Federal Reserve Board's survey of 22,000 people found that the share of people saying that "they are doing at least okay financially" had risen over the last few years to 74 percent of the population. The question was "How are you doing financially?" and provided four answer choices, with the second positive choice being "Doing okay."

For those with a college degree, the positive answers were at 88 percent. When asked about living standards relative to their parents' at the same age, 53 percent said they were better off and most of the other responders said their living standards were the same. The General Social Survey gets similar results for this question. Further, the Pew Research Center regularly polls people on their satisfaction with their lives and finances, and they too have found that a large majority answered positively.

Oddly, polls show an "optimism bias": people like what they personally experience but are critical of the national version of the same theme (see David Whitman's book with this title). For instance, "Congress stinks, but I like my representative" or "I think public schools are bad, but I like the schools that my children attend." Psychologists have argued that we react more to negative events than positive ones, so it is very easy to find fault and take the good for granted. Social media certainly feeds off and intensifies negative feelings.

U.S. manufacturing workers were in a unique position to obtain wage gains and better benefits from 1946 through the 1970s. First, industrial unions had wide public support. Second, the war had destroyed the infrastructure and reduced the workforce of the United States' industrial competitors in Europe and Japan. Third, there was the cycle of economic growth that led to more growth. U.S. firms faced high demands from citizens who were starting new families (the baby boom started in 1946) and needed new houses, cars, and appliances.

By the mid-to-late 1960s, the United States' prized position began to be whittled away. Europe and Japan narrowed the productivity gap and made cars that were attractive to those in the United States. Rising inflation was driven by an expansionary fiscal policy in fighting the Vietnam War without cutting other domestic spending or raising taxes. Many union contracts had cost-of-living adjustment provisions that increased earnings as inflation increased. U.S. companies embraced automation and adopted a more oppositional stance to union demands. Further, many low-paying manufacturing industries changed locations within the United States and, starting in 1964, changed to maquiladoras in Mexico.

There are turning points in history in which recent events combine with older forces to produce large changes; the early 1980s was one of these periods. The events leading to rising inequality, globalization, and increased reliance on market forces (sometimes called "neoliberalism") were:

1. The stagflation of the 1970s, which contributed to high interest rates and a deep recession. When the economy recovered, firms had the opportunity to start anew.

2. The introduction of the IBM PC in 1981, which was one of the first steps in what would become an IT revolution of mass use of computers, cell phones, and the internet, and which led to an explosion of new products and new ways of organizing office work.

3. The evolution of containerization, which helped organize production within global supply chains.

4. The weakening of unions. President Reagan's breaking of the air traffic controllers' strike gave added impetus for states and companies to become more anti-union.

The economy that emerged was very different from the one of the fifties and sixties as the manufacturing employment share declined from 32 percent in 1955 to 20 percent in 1980 and then to 8 percent in 2019. The changes that occurred over the decades were mainly driven by productivity advances, and manufacturing industries that produce goods were much more likely than service industries to have high productivity gains. For example, the American Iron and Steel Institute reports that it took 10.1 hours to produce a ton of steel in 1960 versus 1.5 hours today. As a whole, manufacturing industries did slightly worse, as output per hour grew by just under 600 percent.

While there have always been discussions about the rich and the poor, the first time that researchers collected data to issue reports on changing inequality was in 1980s. Several studies on the fifties and sixties found little change in inequality. One study in the 1970s found rising inequality in male earnings. Many more studies of inequality would follow.

The rise in inequality after 1980 was based on structural changes: the decline in labor power as the share of private workers in unions declined, the decline of the real value of the minimum wage, and trade deficits. Many people focus on outsourcing because imports always seem to displace domestic workers. This is a very simplistic view because it does not account for exports and other international money flows. In the 1960s, autoworkers burned foreign cars at a time when the value of American imports and exports was about the same. Further, the share of imports that came from low-wage countries was low then and not that much higher today. Finally, foreign auto companies, especially Japanese and German, built factories in the southern states. These "transplants" are mostly nonunion and haven't stopped the steady reduction of the manufacturing share of employment.

In a 2021 paper, I show that manufacturing imports grew by $1.9 trillion from 1991 to 2019 while manufacturing exports increased by $1.4 trillion. Using established methods, this monetary difference translates into 9 million lost jobs due to imports and 3.5 million gained jobs. But this number is not large when compared to the size of the labor force (over 150 million) or to the 40 million net gain in the number employed from 1991 to 2019.

Our labor force has many workers entering and leaving jobs—some voluntarily and some involuntarily. According to the Job Openings and Labor Market Turnover Survey, from 2000 (first year of the survey) to 2019, 36 million workers a year voluntarily left their jobs and another 24 million workers per year were either laid off or discharged. In contrast, the yearly manufacturing loss due to imports was 310,000 a year.

Finally, the net loss of 3.5 million jobs due to trade represents a small share of the additional 26 million manufacturing jobs that would have existed if the manufacturing employment share of the labor force remained at its 1960 level. Trade does have an effect on jobs and rising labor compensation inequality, but the effect is not large. In the end, the main determinants of the size of the labor force are larger macro factors, government spending and taxation, and the actions of the Federal Reserve Board.

Trade's effect on manufacturing workers' earnings starts with the fallacy of the "family wage"—the ability of the male factory worker to support a wife and two children at a comfortable level on his salary alone. It was true that workers in several prominent unions did have high enough salaries to do this, but workers in many other industries, such as textiles, shoes, and clothing, had much lower wages. Since I have never seen a study on the family wage, I define a reasonable wage for machine operators in manufacturing as yearly earnings above the fortieth percentile of the overall male full-time, full-year earners. I found that 56 percent of manufacturing workers met this definition in 1960 versus 42 percent in 2014. The effect of trade on earnings inequality is small because relative earnings were down a bit while the share of manufacturing workers was much lower.

In terms of changes in our economic structure, governmental industrial categories have agriculture, mining, and manufacturing as "goods production" while everything else is considered services. For many people, services connote low-skilled jobs, such as flipping burgers, cleaning hotel rooms, and working in retail. But virtually all high-paying jobs for those with college and graduate degrees—e.g., doctors, lawyers, bankers, engineers, professors, and K–12 teachers—are service workers. The rising premium on four-year college degrees is based on the growth of business professionals and the IT revolution.

I have identified five main "functions" based on the type of work done rather than the output of companies:

* Agriculture, including fishing
* Manual labor in manufacturing, construction, and mining
* Low-skilled services and retail workers
* Non-administrative workers in health care, education, and communication

* Office work, including front office workers in manufacturing and other industries

The first two functions consist of manual workers producing goods. This leaves three service functions—one low-skilled and two high-skilled. The high-skilled service functions dominate the current U.S. economy, representing 67 percent of employment and 75 percent of cash earnings (they have high pay, 81 percent have a four-year degree, and 91 percent have a graduate degree, based on March 2020 data).

The employment share of these five functions changed dramatically from 1980 to 2019:

* Agriculture declined from 6 percent to 1 percent
* Manual labor declined even more, from 30 percent to 16 percent
* Surprisingly, low-skilled services fell from 20 percent to 16 percent
* Health care and education more than doubled its share from 10 percent to 21 percent
* Office work gained 11 percentage points, going from 34 percent to 45 percent

The last two categories are high-end services. The large share of employment in offices, health care, and education should not surprise anyone given the large buildings that dominate central cities and even suburbs. The large office function consists of three activities:

* Administration, strategic planning, and sales promotion for manufacturing and other industries
* Government administration, planning, and services (including legislatures, courts, prisons, law enforcement, sanitation, and firefighters)
* Financial and professional services to government, companies, and individuals

The high-end service workers in offices, health care, and education are the main employer of those with a four-year or graduate degree—81 percent of those with a four-year degree and 91 percent of those with a graduate degree work in these jobs. Some do intellectual and analytical work; others do not. Some skills require very specific training; others require general literacy, communication, and simple analytical skills. And there is a cadre of supporting clerical and other workers whose jobs do not require a college degree.

The shift of these changes is mirrored in the changes of the types of jobs. In my 2010 book, I describe a three-tier categorization (based on aggregation of twenty-one subcategories):

* Elite jobs: all managers and professionals
* Good jobs: supervisors, skilled blue-collar and craft workers, technicians, police, firefighters, and clerical workers
* Less-skilled jobs: blue-collar machine operators and laborers, sales clerks, and personal and food-service workers.

Contrary to many claims about the growth in low-skilled services, the quality of employment in America has been shifting upward during the past forty years. In 1960, almost one-half of the workforce (44 percent) was in less-skilled positions and only 18 percent held elite jobs. The occupation chapter (chapter 5) shows the upskilling of independent adults from 1979 to 2019, while the education chapter (chapter 4) documents the big rise of people with college degrees.

Another consequence of the advancement in productivity involves what Americans consume (Figure 15). Productivity gains are highest in the production of goods. Consequently, the categories with the largest declines are food (down 13 percentage points), clothing (down 6 points), personal and household goods (down 4 points), and transportation (down 3 points). The biggest areas of gain were health and education (up 16.5 percentage

FIGURE 15

Share of
consumption
by type:
1959, 2019

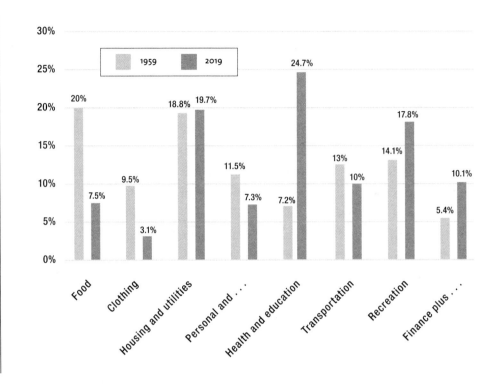

Source: Author's
computation from the
Bureau of Economics,
Natation Income and
Product Accounts Table

points), recreation, and finance and personal business services (up 5 points).

As a consequence of these structural changes, the earnings of college grads and graduate-degree holders have grown significantly versus those of lesser-educated workers. Economists call these movements "skill-biased technological change." As Figure 16 shows, the "BA premium" over those with just a high school diploma and no postsecondary education grew from 45 percent in 1960 to 82 percent in 2019. Further, those with a graduate degree saw their advantage over those with just a four-year degree go from 21 percent in 1980 to 33 percent in 2019.

Other forces that increase inequality:

＊ Declining unionization certainly had a big negative effect on manufacturing wages. While some argue that the threat of moving facilities overseas has been used as an effective tactic to keep wages low, companies' attacks on unions predate the jump in international trade. In 1973, manufacturing unionization was at 38 percent; half of the decline in manufacturing unionization occurred from 1973 to 1985, when trade deficits were small. From 1986 through 2019 unionization rates declined steadily to 8 percent while the trade deficit had big swings.

＊ The real value of the minimum wage kept up with inflation from the time it was enacted in 1938 through 1968, when it was a bit higher than $10 per hour in 2019 dollars. However, since 1968, the minimum wage has not kept up with inflation and has been stuck at $7.25 per hour since 2009. Oddly, legislators originally resisted tying the minimum wage to inflation because they wanted to take credit for raising the minimum wage. In the last forty years, there have been few

FIGURE 16

Rising
educational
premiums

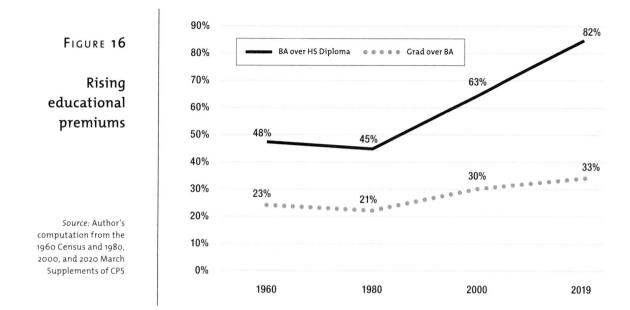

Source: Author's
computation from the
1960 Census and 1980,
2000, and 2020 March
Supplements of CPS

minimum wage increases The Congressional Budget Office estimated that 17 million workers would have higher earnings if the minimum wage was set at $15; another 10 million with hourly wages just above the current level would also benefit.

✳ Immigration, both legal and illegal, has increased the supply of low-skilled workers. This factor is combined in many people's mind with trade deficits because they both depend on foreign actors. Yet a major study from the National Academy of Sciences found no evidence that immigrant workers decrease the pay of any group of American workers.

Conclusion

THE FIRST EDITION OF THE POSTER IN 1979 portrayed high income inequality. Little did I expect that inequality would get progressively worse. The second edition of the poster changed the focus from the bottom half of the income ladder to the middle class. The headline finding was that the middle class had shrunk. This finding was received as one of the first research reports documenting growing inequality. Lost from the dire headlines were two caveats: 1983 was preceded by the double-dip recession of 1980 to 1982, and almost as many people moved up out of the middle class as moved down.

After the second edition, including this one, the posters showed rising real incomes across the income ladder and rising inequality. As Figure 8 shows, the 2019 distribution is always higher than the 1979 distribution, and the gap between the two lines grows as incomes rise. This is very true at the ninetieth and ninety-fifth percentiles, where 2019 incomes are much higher than the 1979 comparable percentiles. These findings of modest gains in median incomes differ from the widely cited findings of Piketty and Saez of declining median incomes from 1979. Their first paper came out in 2003 and was updated yearly through 2017. In 2017, however, they produced (with Gabriel Zucman) a new study with a different methodology that found that median incomes had grown over 35 percent from 1979 to 2016.

The confusion surrounding the term "middle class" shows that we must take special care in defining terms and distinguishing various groups within the population before we can have an informed debate about pressing social issues. For instance, data on the poster and in the figures and tables in this book reveal the significant presence of many different social and ethnic groups in the $74,000–$111,000 income range. This income group includes approximately the same number of managerial/professional workers as middle- and low-skilled blue-, white-, and pink-collar workers.

There are three types of inequality. First, there are people stuck in low to moderate incomes. Many whites in this group feel that affirmative action is unfair. Over half of this group (often not living in urban areas) say that whites are more discriminated against than blacks. The second type of inequality consists of noncollege people with moderate incomes who feel talked down to by college-educated members of the upper middle class. In particular, they feel that technocrats, government workers, and college teachers don't do real work.

The third kind of inequality consists of those with the high incomes and wealth of the top 1 percent. The Piketty study shone a critical light on the plutocrats and billionaires—the top one-hundredth of 1 percent. However, while there is support for raising taxes on the rich, super wealthy candidates without any previous political experience have been elected to high-level positions. Further, opinion polls show that over 60 percent of the public are against inheritance taxes even if the tax applies only to estates over $12 million. There is a sense that people "earned" their money even if they have great wealth—e.g., entertainers, athletes, or famous entrepreneurs such as Bill Gates, Mark Zuckerberg, and Michael Dell.

The world is complex and polarized more intensely than in the five decades following World War II. We tend to follow the leaders of our tribe while being closed to statements by experts of the other side. The purpose of this poster and book, however limited a picture of contemporary society it may be, is to make information more accessible. Hopefully, this work will stimulate thought and more questions and arm the reader with more skills in understanding issues and the data that support each side.

Appendix I

Suggestions for Classroom Use

THE POSTER PROVIDES AN OPPORTUNITY TO involve students directly in developing social analysis. After a brief introduction about the meaning of the symbols and colors, students should be encouraged to study and discuss the poster in groups of six to ten.

The first tendency is to find one's family on the poster, which may lead to the negative dynamic of students' comparing themselves and boasting about their relative status. This should be discouraged by having each student write anonymously the occupations of his or her parents and family income. The teacher can put this information on the blackboard and try to focus the discussion on the class taken as a whole rather than on individual circumstances. Even this may create problems, though: students may not know their family's income, and parents may question the validity of a classroom exercise that has their children coming home asking potentially sensitive questions.

That young people have little understanding of how high various living expenses run—another potential problem—can be turned to advantage by having them create family budgets as an initial exercise. To make up worksheets, teachers can consult the Consumer Expenditure Survey to find how much households at different income levels spend on twenty-five different types of purchases.

If a teacher does decide to poll the class anonymously, an income line from $0 to $300,000 can be drawn on the blackboard and an X used to mark off each student's family income. Then the distribution of class can be compared to the shape on the poster or one of the figures in the text. In most cases, the class's distribution will be much more concentrated than that of society at large. Depending on the results, the teacher can draw the appropriate conclusions. For example, most wealthy suburban communities consider themselves to be "upper middle class." They may be shocked to see that incomes in the $100,000–$250,000 range put them in rather limited company in relation to the whole population. The counterexample of a class from a poor neighborhood should be treated with care so as to avoid feelings of shame at placing low on the poster.

Once the class has developed a sense of itself, other exercises can involve picking different parts of town and fitting typical families from those places on the poster. Another possibility involves assigning six different households from different parts of the poster to separate groups of students. Each group can then be responsible for describing in greater depth the social conditions of that household.

Most of these exercises involve focusing on the vertical dimension of the poster. To emphasize the horizontal aspect, one can look at a given income range and compare the various households that make it up. In fact, families with the same income often live quite differently, with different expectations and lifestyles. Once again, students can learn more about society by actively studying its diversity. Other projects can target specific subgroups: retired people, women, blacks, one of the occupational categories, and so on. Tracing paper can be used to mark the appropriate figures, and then the pattern of X's on the tracing paper can be compared with the shape of the poster or to other traced shapes.

Other projects can focus on groups—for example, union workers—that may not be identified on the poster; students will have to ascertain which poster figures would be the appropriate match for the studied group.

Another possibility is to make international comparisons or comparisons over time. The class may wish to construct a picture of the United States in 1950, 1900, and 1850. Here, the problem of data availability becomes quite difficult because the decennial censuses (available in many large libraries) contain little detailed economic information before 1950. Some information is available, though, and doing original library research may be challenging. A good place to begin is the Census's *Historical Statistics: Colonial Times to 1970*. Should a teacher try this exercise, it will quickly become clear how much information is necessary to construct a picture as complete as that presented on the poster. For other countries, the World Bank, Organization for Economic Development, and CIA publish a series of data books and individual national reports. Finally, the Luxembourg Income study has raw data from income studies from fifty countries for multiple years,

These suggestions are only a starting point in the effort to involve students in caring about their social environment and trying to understand it. Within each exercise, there can be discussion of why things have developed in this fashion— particularly in the case of historical comparisons. All of this opens the door to questions about politics and citizenship. Thus, one can try to figure out which social groups support which party, push for new legislation, or take part in other forms of social action, such as demonstrations and forming organizations.

All of these activities will be possible if the students become involved with the poster and learn to identify history and social relations as tangible rather than abstract. By making one set of statistics accessible, the poster can heighten curiosity and give a sense of power to students to investigate other areas because they have a new way to understand them.

Appendix II

References and Public Data Sources

Government Reports

Most of the data are currently available through the websites of each agency.

Overview

Department of Commerce, Bureau of the Census
Statistical Abstract (annual)
City and County Data Book
United States Congress, House of Representatives, Committee on Ways and Means, *Data on Programs Under the Jurisdiction of the Committee on Ways and Means* (annual)
Department of Education, *Digest of Educational Statistics* (annual)
The President of the United States, *Economic Report of the President* (annual)

Production, Prices, Income, and Employment

Bureau of the Census
   Business Conditions Digest (monthly)
   Survey of Current Business (monthly)
   County Business Patterns (annual)
Bureau of Labor Statistics
   Monthly Review
   Employment and Earnings (monthly)
Federal Reserve Bank, *Federal Reserve Bulletin* (monthly)
Internal Revenue Service, *Statistics of Income* (quarterly)
Social Security Administration, *Social Security Bulletin* (monthly)

Special Report Series

Bureau of the Census, Current Population Reports
P-60 Series, on Income and Poverty
P-20 Series, on Household Composition
P-70 Series, on Wealth, Education, and Special Studies
Bureau of Labor Statistics, Special Labor Force bulletins

Appendix III

Other Published Works by the Author

"Do Not Blame Trade for the Decline in Manufacturing Jobs." Center for Strategic and International Studies, 2021.

"The Upper Middle Class Continued to Grow from 2014 to 2019." Urban Institute, 2021.

"The Growth of the Office Economy: Underrecognized Sector in High-Income Economies." *Critical Sociology* 47 (4/5), 2021, 795–805.

"The Ins and Outs of Measuring Income Inequality in the United States." In *United States Trends in Income, Wealth, Consumption, and Inequality.* Edited by Diana Furchtgott-Roth. New York: Oxford University Press, 2020.

"What Do College-Educated Workers Do? Answering This Question Is the Key to Understanding Modern Economies Across the Globe." Urban Institute, 2021.

"Life-Cycle Income Trajectories, 1967 to 2016." Brookings Institution. 2020.

"How Different Studies Measure Income Inequality the U.S.: Piketty and Company Aren't the Only Game in Town." Urban Institute. December 2018.

"Measuring Income Inequality in the U.S.: Methodological Issues." Urban Institute. December 2018.

"Still a Man's Labor Market: The Slowly Narrowing Gender Wage Gap." Washington, DC: Institute for Women's Policy Research. November 2018.

"America Goes to College: The Hidden Promise of Higher Education in the Postindustrial Service Economy." With Anthony Carnevale. Georgetown Center on Education and Workforce. 2014.

"The Value of a College Degree." *Change: The Magazine of Higher Learning* 45, no. 6, 24–33.

"Certificates: The Gateway to Gainful Employment and College Degrees." With Anthony Carnevale. Georgetown Center on Education and Workforce. June 2012.

"The College Payoff: Education, Occupations, and Lifetime Earnings." With Anthony Carnevale. Georgetown Center on Education and Workforce. September 2011.

"The Undereducated American." With Anthony Carnevale. Georgetown Center on Education and Workforce. June 2011.

Rebound: Why America Will Emerge Stronger from the Financial Crisis. New York: St. Martin's Press, April 2010.

"Ups and Downs: Does the American Economy Still Promote Upward Mobility?" With Scott Winship. Pew Economic Mobility Project. June 2009.

"Blinder Baloney: Today's Scare Talk of Job Outsourcing Is Grossly Exaggerated." With William Dickens. *International Economy*, October 2007.

"Does Productivity Growth Still Benefit Working Americans? Unraveling the Income Growth Mystery to Determine How Much Median Incomes Trail Productivity Growth." Information Technology and Innovation Foundation. June 2007.

"Talking Past the Middle," *Challenge*, January 2007. A version of this article was the centerpiece of "Debating the Middle" organized by the editors of *American Prospect*, www.prospect.org/cs/debates_chat.

"Still a Man's Labor Market: The Long-Term Earnings Gap." With Heidi Hartmann. Institute for Women's Policy Research. 2004. Reprinted in a condensed version as "The Long-Term Gender Gap." *Challenge* 47, no. 5, 2004. 30–50.

"Socioeconomic Status, Race/Ethnicity, and Selective College Admissions." With Anthony Carnevale. In *America's Untapped Resource: Low-Income Students in Higher Education*. Edited by Richard Kahlenberg. Century Foundation. 2003.

"The Challenge of Measuring Earnings Mobility and Career Paths in the United States." *Indicators: the Journal of Social Health* 1, no. 4, 2002. 73–98.

"Inequality in the New High-Skilled Service Economy." With Anthony Carnevale. In *Unconventional Wisdom: New Perspectives in Economics*. Edited by Jeff Madrick. Century Foundation. 2000.

Acknowledgments

MANY TEACHERS AND COMMENTATORS have used various visual images to portray disparities in the distribution of income in the United States—for example, a marching band that takes an hour to pass the viewing stand of the Eiffel Tower. In the early 1970s, sociologist Jan Houbolt solicited the graphic assistance of Dennis Livingston to create a 100-figure chart with managers, teachers, carpenters, and other occupational categories. The purpose was to personalize mathematical relations that students often comprehended only vaguely.

In 1978 Livingston and I expanded this initial idea to create a statistically accurate 1,000-figure portrayal of the American social structure. With money raised from friends, the Social Graphics Company was formed to produce the original *Social Stratification in the United States* poster and guidebook. After the first edition and a 1980 reprint were sold out, a new edition was created in 1983. Kathryn Shagas took over the artistic presentation and redesigned the icons and layout. Interest and sales continued, leading Tom Engelhardt, then an editor at Pantheon Books, to commission a 1986 update with a changed title, *The American Profile Poster*.

In 1992, the next updated edition was published by The New Press, and the original title was restored. After updates in 2000, 2014 and 2007, this poster and booklet represent the eighth edition of the original 1978 concept. The poster continues to represent the clearest and most succinct picture of America's social structure, providing a basis for tracking social change over the past thirty-five years. This edition benefited from the editorial assistance of Ben Woodward, managing editorial help of Maury Botton, copy editing by Cathy Dexter, and book design and composition by Brian Mulligan.